KIDS' MICROWAVE
STEP-BY-STEP RECIPES

MARY PAT FERGUS

MURDOCH BOOKS
Sydney • London • Vancouver

The Publisher thanks the following for their assistance:

Corso De'Fiori
House & Garden
Etcetera
Horgan Imports
Pillivuyt
St John Ambulance
Villeroy and Boch
Sharp Corporation of Australia Pty Ltd

All recipes in this book can be made by
a child with little or no help from an adult.
All the microwave recipes have been
tested in a 600-700 watt microwave.
Each recipe is set out to make cooking
simple.

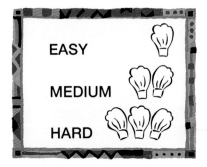

EASY

MEDIUM

HARD

Recipes are graded to help you learn. If
you are just starting out to cook you might
prefer to try the recipes marked easy (1
chef's hat); when you have a little exper-
ience, try medium (2 chef's hats) and
when you are more experienced try hard
(3 chef's hats) recipes.

Front cover: Funny Face and Gingerbread Man (page 96-97)

Back cover: Pavlova (page 71)

Frontispiece: Custard (page 54)

CONTENTS

Microwave cooking is great fun, we've made it easy too with our step-by-step recipes. Before you start micro cooking read over these next pages to learn a little more about the special equipment and techniques you need to know to make every recipe a success. Take time to get organised. Read over the recipe thoroughly, read it all the way through and check that you have all the ingredients. Collect everything you need for your recipe — all the ingredients and all the equipment.

If your recipe calls for chopped or shredded ingredients, do this before you begin. Also open any cans and wash any vegetables or fruits. Grease any microwave cookware if you need to.

All the recipes are set out in easy to follow step-by-step form. Remember to finish each step before beginning the next one.

IMPORTANT SAFETY POINTS

Here are a few hints and tips to make micro cooking safe and enjoyable.

✓ Always ask an adult for permission before you start.
✓ Before starting to cook, wash your hands well with soap and water. Wear an apron to protect your clothes and wear closed-in, non-slip shoes to protect your feet.
✓ Collect everything you need for your recipe before you start — all the ingredients and the necessary kitchen equipment.
✓ Unless you are allowed to use knives, ask an adult to help you chop things. Never cut directly on a kitchen surface — always use a chopping board. When you are using a knife pick it up by the handle, not by the blade. Keep your fingers well clear of the blade when chopping foods.
✓ Take care when washing knives, too. Keep the sharp edge of the blade away from you and store the knives out of reach of any young brothers or sisters.
✓ Always use oven mitts to remove dishes from the microwave oven. Remember that anything you take from the microwave oven will be hot for a while.
✓ Take great care when you uncover foods from the microwave oven, so that the steam won't burn you. Lift the far side of the cover up first, letting the steam go up and out away from you. Use tongs when you are removing cling wrap.
✓ When stirring microwave dishes, hold the container with oven mitts as you stir.
✓ Never operate the microwave oven without food inside.

✓ Most importantly, clean up the kitchen when you have finished cooking. Put away all the ingredients and the equipment you have used. Wash the dishes — start with washing the least soiled dishes like glassware and bowls and then do the microwave cookware. Dry the dishes thoroughly and put them back in their place. Wipe down your work surface with a clean cloth and then I'm sure, you'll be allowed to cook again another day.

First Aid for Burns and Scalds

Cool the burnt parts with cold water for at least ten minutes. Make the hurt person comfortable, but do not move them if the burn or scald is serious. Protect against infection by covering the burns or scalds with clean non-adherent material. Do not touch. Do not remove stuck clothing.

Always use oven mitts to remove cooked dishes from the microwave oven.

Take care when you uncover food from the microwave oven, food will be hot.

When stirring microwave dishes, hold the container with oven mitts as you stir.

MICROWAVE KNOW HOW

All microwave ovens are different, before beginning to cook get to know a little about your microwave oven. You may need to ask an adult to help you.

✓ Firstly, find out what wattage your microwave oven is — this is important to determine cooking times. All our recipes were tested in a 600 to 700 watt microwave. If yours has fewer watts foods will take a little longer to cook.

✓ Learn how to operate or set your microwave oven from High to Low and how to set the timer. To follow are the temperatures and percentages we used:
High: 100% power
Medium High: 75% power
Medium: 50 % power
Low: 30% power

✓ When cooking with a microwave oven you will find that some foods cook a little more quickly than others in a particular dish. These foods need stirring as they cook, so that they cook evenly.

✓ Place microwave dishes in the centre of the microwave oven unless otherwise stated.

✓ In microwave cooking food is often covered, use the lid of the microwave dish or microwave cling wrap. Take great care when removing the lid or cling wrap to avoid burning yourself.

MICRO COOK'S TOOLS

There are many tools used in the kitchen to make micro cooking easy. There are wooden and micro safe spoons to stir with, spatulas to combine ingredients, bowls of varying sizes to mix things in, strainers or colanders to drain and rinse foods in, racks or micro dishes to elevate dishes in the oven, and micro dishes to cook

CONTAINERS TO USE IN THE MICROWAVE OVEN

• Lots of special microwave containers are made out of plastic but before you use them, look underneath the dish to make sure it tells you how it can be used. Some say they are suitable for most things but not for foods with lots of fat, oil or sugar. These get very, very hot and if you're not using a suitable plastic dish, the heat could damage or even make it melt!

• **Do not use any metal containers in the microwave.**

• Don't use any dishes, plates, mugs or cups that have a silver or gold trim. These metals react badly with microwaves. The nice trim could turn a nasty colour or, more important, they may cause sparks that could damage the oven.

• Don't *ever* use fine bone china, crystal bowls or glasses.

• Some pottery mugs or casseroles dishes have a glaze that contains small amounts of metal. These can get very hot in the oven and could give you a nasty burn.

• The best containers to use, especially if cooking with liquid, are those with a handle for safe removal from the microwave

oven. Don't forget — the oven might feel fairly cool, but the dish could be hot, so have some oven mitts ready.

To see if plastic containers or dishes you're not sure about are safe to use, here's a simple test to tell you what to do:

1 Put the empty suspicious container in the oven along with a 'safe' mug or bowl of water and turn on the power to High (100%) for 1½ minutes.

2 If the water in the 'safe' mug is cool and the 'suspicious' container is hot, then it must *never* be used in the microwave.

3 If the water is warm and the 'suspicious' container is cool, it's OK to use it in the oven.

4 If the 'suspicious' container is slightly warm, it can be used for a short time in the oven — maybe to heat up a piece of pie — but not for longer periods.

things in. Use absorbent paper, cling wrap and wax paper to cover ingredients while microwaving. Then there are wire racks for cooling cakes and cookies, metal spatulas to help you measure and also to spread ingredients or toppings evenly over foods.

The recipes in this book use only basic equipment found in most kitchens. If in doubt about any equipment you may need to ask an adult for some help.

SOME SIMPLE MICROWAVE COOKING TERMS

BEAT: Stir foods with a spoon or electric mixer until they are smooth.

CHOP: Cut food carefully into small pieces. To chop finely is to cut foods as small as you can.

COVER: Make sure you do 'cover' when the recipe tells you to or food might dry out. But also, don't forget to leave off the lid or cling wrap when the recipe says 'cook uncovered', because a cover *on* that should not be on could cause a 'boil-over' in the microwave oven.

DEFROST: Allow food to slowly defrost, otherwise you could have a chicken with cooked wings and raw thighs. It's OK to use small pieces of aluminium foil to protect the thin parts of meats, fish and poultry. Wrap a small, smooth piece of foil around the thin part but make sure the foil does not touch the walls of the oven. Defrosting or thawing out frozen meat, fish or chicken should never be done more than once.

DRAIN: Strain away unwanted liquid using a colander or strainer. Do this over the kitchen sink so that water can drain away down the sink.

GRATE: Rub food against a grater. Do this over absorbent paper. Hold the grater with one hand and rub the food back and forth over the grating holes. This gives you long thin pieces. For finely grated foods use the smallest grating holes.

GREASE: Brush micro containers and cooking utensils with melted butter, margarine or oil to stop foods sticking when you microwave them.

KNEAD: Lightly rub or mould foods like pastry or scone dough on a floured surface until smooth and pliable.

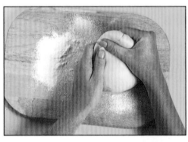

MASH: Squash cooked or very ripe foods with a fork or potato masher.

PIERCE: This is when you pierce the cling wrap cover in several places with a fork to avoid liquid boiling over.

RACKS: These are used for elevating (or lifting) dishes up a little from the tray in the bottom of the oven. This helps cakes and some desserts to cook more evenly. It you don't have a microwave rack, you can use a small, upturned saucer or dish to lift up the food a little.

REST or ALLOW TO STAND: Means that the food should be taken from the oven, covered and set aside so that the small amount of extra cooking after microwaving is finished can take place. For example, if you cook something rather delicate such as fish, until it's completely cooked, it may be a little over-done by the time you're ready to eat it. It is far better to remove it from the oven when it's almost cooked, cover it for a minute or two then eat it when it's 'just right'.

SCRAPE: Lightly peel or remove skin from vegetables like carrots using a small kitchen knife.

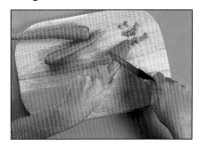

SEPARATING EGGS: When egg whites or yolks are required for a recipe. Hold the egg over a small plate and carefully crack the shell with a metal spatula or table knife. Let the egg fall out onto the plate, place a small glass over the yolk and then carefully tip the white into a bowl. If any yolk gets into the white, you can easily remove it with a piece of eggshell.

SLICE: Cut foods like apples, carrots and tomatoes into thin rounds or sections.

STERILISING JARS: Jars for storing jams and chutney must be sterilised to prevent the growth of moulds. Clean jars very well in hot water, warm jars in a conventional oven at about 150°C, remove the jars from the oven with oven mitts and use the jars straight from the oven when you need them. Ask an adult to help you as the jam or chutney mixture will be very hot!

STIR: We say this a lot when microwaving, because if we don't stir liquid regularly, the outside of the food gets hot, while the middle is only slightly warm.

WHISK: Mix ingredients together with a balloon shaped utensil by moving in a circular motion until combined or smooth.

COOKED INGREDIENTS

Some of the recipes in this book call for cooked ingredients — the following will help you prepare these extras.

COOKED RICE: Place a large pan of water on the stove to boil, add the rice to the steadily boiling water, stir in carefully and cook for 8 – 12 minutes or until tender. You may need to ask an adult to help you drain it in a colander or strainer over the sink. Use immediately for hot dishes or rinse well with cold water and cool for cold dishes.

HARD BOILED EGGS: Place a small pan of water on the stove to boil, when water boils use a spoon to lower eggs into boiling water, take care. Boil for about 10 minutes, lift eggs out with tongs or a slotted spoon, run cold water over them and peel immediately.

ICINGS: For a quick and easy Lemon Icing: Sift one cup of icing sugar into a bowl that's standing in bowl of hot water. Stir in 2 tablespoons of lemon juice until mixture is smooth. Pour over the cooled cake, smooth top with a knife dipped in hot water if needed. For Chocolate Icing: Sift in 1 tablespoon of cocoa with the icing sugar and replace the lemon juice with hot water.

SKINNING TOMATOES: This is easy with a little practice, simply cut a small cross at the base of the tomato, place it in a bowl. Pour over boiling water, wait for 1 minute, lift out tomato with a slotted spoon. Starting at the cross carefully peel away the skin, use as directed in the recipe.

WHIPPING CREAM: Place about 1 cup of cream in a glass or ceramic bowl, use a whisk or a hand beater to slowly whip the cream into soft peaks, take care not to overbeat it.

MEASURING UP

Careful measuring of your ingredients makes for a successful recipe. You will need a set of dry measuring cups, which usually come in a set of four: a 1 cup measure, ½ cup, ⅓ cup and

¼ cup measure. These are used to measure ingredients like flour and sugar. You will also need a liquid measuring cup that usually has a lip for easy pouring and lines on the side that mark the different liquid measures. Milk, water and juice are measured with this cup.

Measuring spoons will also be needed to measure small amounts. They are marked and measure 1 tablespoon, 1 teaspoon, ½ teaspoons and ¼ teaspoon.

DRY MEASURES

Take care to use the correct size measuring cup as stated in the recipe, especially if you are baking cakes or cookies. Spoon the dry ingredients lightly into the measuring cup and level it off with a metal spatula. It's a good idea to do this over a piece of absorbent paper to avoid any mess.

In some recipes you will need to do some simple maths to get the correct amount you need. For example, you may need ⅔ cup flour for a recipe, so simply measure out ⅓ cup using correct measure and then another ⅓ cup and add both to the recipe.

Brown sugar is measured as a dry ingredient and you will need to pack it down tightly in the measuring cup, filling it until it is level with the top of the cup.

You will probably find that you need to run a metal spatula around the cup to loosen the sugar.

Level dry ingredients with a spatula.

LIQUID MEASURES

To measure a liquid ingredient place the liquid measuring cup on the bench or board, add some of the liquid and bend down so that your eyes are level with the measurement marks. Check to see if you have enough liquid; if necessary pour in a little more. If you have too much liquid simply pour out the extra.

SPOON MEASURES

Measuring spoons are different from the spoons you use for eating. They are used to measure small amounts.

To measure liquid choose the correct size spoon for the amount you need and carefully pour the liquid into the bowl of the spoon. It's a good idea to hold the spoon over a cup or jug to avoid spills.

To measure dry ingredients fill the correct spoon with your dry ingredients and then carefully level off the amount with a metal spatula.

BUTTER AND MARGARINE

Butter and margarine are generally measured in grams. You will find that blocks of butter have a weight marking on the side of the wrapper. Use a small knife to cut through the butter at the correct marking and then unwrap it. Butter and margarine may also be weighed using a kitchen scale.

Use weight marking on wrapper.

Place measuring cup on flat surface.

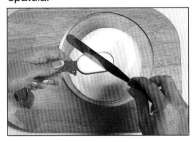

Spoon to measure small amounts.

Or weigh quantity on a kitchen scale.

CHAPTER ONE

SOUPS

Super tasty soups that are sure to tempt all the family. Perfect as a starter or a quick and easy meal. Serve them with lots of Garlic Bread.

CHICKEN CHOWDER

Serves 4

2 slices bacon, rind removed
1 onion
1 potato, peeled + cut into small cubes
1 cup canned whole kernel corn, drained

3 cups hot water
3 teaspoons chicken stock powder
1 cup chopped cooked chicken
¼ cup milk
¼ cup chopped parsley

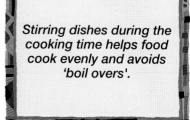

Stirring dishes during the cooking time helps food cook evenly and avoids 'boil overs'.

Finely chop bacon. Peel + finely chop onion. Put in 2 litre casserole.

Cover with cling wrap. Cook on Medium (50%) 5 minutes.

Stir in potato, corn, hot water + chicken stock.

Cover. Cook on High for 10 minutes.

Stir well. Stir in the cooked chicken.

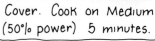

Cover. Cook on Medium (50% power) 5 minutes.

Take off cover. Cook on Medium (50%) 5 minutes more.

Stir in milk and parsley and serve.

VEGETABLE SOUP

Serves 4

1 onion, finely chopped
1 potato, peeled + grated
1 carrot, grated
1 cup grated pumpkin
1 zucchini, grated
1 tomato, skinned +
   chopped
2½ cups hot water
2½ teaspoons chicken
   stock powder
2 tablespoons chopped
   parsley
1 teaspoon soy sauce
ground pepper

Always use oven mitts to remove dishes from the microwave oven. Anything you take from the microwave will stay hot for a while.

1 Put onion, potato, carrot, pumpkin, zucchini, tomato in big bowl 24cm wide, 12cm deep.

2  Add 1 cup of the hot water, and chicken stock. Cover with cling wrap.

3 Cook on High for 10 minutes, stirring once.

4  Stir in remaining hot water, parsley, soy sauce, pepper.

5 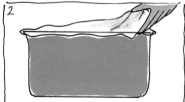 Cover. Cook on Medium High (75% power) 10 minutes.

6  Take out, let it cool down for a while. Stir.

7  Blend it until smooth. Put back in bowl.

8  Reheat - about 3 minutes on High and serve.

SEAFOOD CHOWDER

Serves 4

1 rasher of bacon
1 onion
1 medium potato
1 carrot
3 medium tomatoes
1½ cups chopped white fish fillets

2 cups hot water
1½ cups cooked seafood mix
¼ cup choped parsley
ground pepper
¼ cup milk

1. Finely chop bacon + onion Peel + chop potato. Grate carrot.

2. Put in big bowl about 24 cm wide and 12 cm deep.

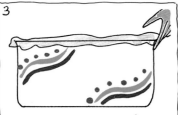

3. Cover with cling wrap. Cook on High 5 minutes. Stir it.

4. Skin + chop tomatoes Add to bowl.

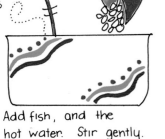

5. Add fish, and the hot water. Stir gently.

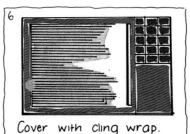

6. Cover with cling wrap. Cook on High 6 minutes.

7. Stir in seafood mix, parsley and pepper.

8. Cover, cook on High 4 minutes. Stir in milk and serve.

FRENCH ONION SOUP

Serves 4

3 onions
1 tablespoon brown sugar
25 g butter
1 tablespoon plain flour
2 beef stock cubes

1½ cups hot water
another 1 cup hot water
4 slices Cheddar cheese
4 slices French bread,
  toasted

The toasted bread and micro melted cheese from this delicious soup recipe make ideal after school snacks.

1. Slice onions. Put in big bowl. Add brown sugar + butter.

2. Cover with cling wrap. Pierce. Cook on High 2½ minutes.

3. Add flour, crumbled stock cubes, 1½ cups hot water. Stir.

4. Cover. Pierce. Cook on High for 10 minutes. Stir.

5. Add the 1 cup hot water.

6. Put cheese on toasted bread on a plate.

7. Cook on High 30 seconds till cheese melts.

8. Put soup in 4 bowls. Float toast on top.   Serve.

TUNA CHOWDER

Serves 4

45g pkt Pea & Ham Soup
1 small onion
3¼ cups hot water
185 g tin tuna, in brine
¾ cup cooked rice
2 tablespoons chopped
   parsley
¼ cup cream

1. Put soup into a big, deep, (24 cm wide) bowl.

2. Peel + finely chop onion. Put in the bowl.

3. Add the hot water. Whisk well.

4. Cook on High for 10 minutes, whisking twice.

5. Drain + flake tuna. Stir it into soup.

6. Add rice + parsley. Stir well.

7. Cook it on High for 5 minutes.

8. Stir in the cream and serve.

CHAPTER TWO

VEGETABLES

Looking for a side dish for dinner, well you're sure to find one that suits in this exciting chapter. Fresh, full-of-flavour vegetable dishes, that taste good and are good for you.

BUTTERED CARROTS

Serves 4

4 medium size carrots
30 g butter
1½ teaspoons French
   mustard
1 teaspoon brown sugar
1 tablespoon chopped
   parsley

1

Wash + scrape carrots.
Slice into thin rounds.

2

Put into a flat round
dish.

3

Chop butter. Dot it
over carrots.

4

Stir in the mustard.
Sprinkle sugar over.

5

Cover dish with cling
wrap. Pierce.

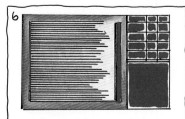

6

Cook it on High for
5 minutes.

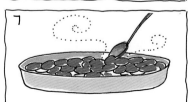

7

Carefully uncover + stir.
Cover dish again.

8

Cook on High 3½ minutes
Stir in parsley. Serve.

CARROTS & ZUCCHINI

Serves 4

3 carrots
2 zucchini
2 tablespoons water
1 tablespoon chopped
   parsley
50 g butter
ground pepper

1
Wash + scrape carrots. Wash + dry zucchini.

2
Cut into very thin strips (like matches) about 5 cm long

3
Put carrots + water into a 20 cm casserole.

4
Cover with cling wrap. Pierce. Cook on High 3 minutes.

5
Stir in zucchini and parsley.

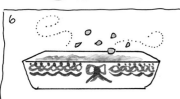

6
Chop up butter and put it on top.

7
Grind pepper on top. Cover with cling wrap. Pierce.

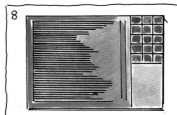

8
Cook on High 3 minutes. Stir and serve.

BAKED ONIONS

Serves 6

3 medium size onions
30 g butter
2 tablespoons tomato sauce
ground pepper
1 tablespoon honey
3 teaspoons sweet paprika
2 tablespoons chopped
  parsley

1. Peel onions. Cut them in half across grain.

2. Put them, cut side down, in a round dish.

3. Put butter, tomato sauce, pepper honey + paprika in a bowl.

4. Cook on High for 1 minute.

5. Stir well + pour over the onions.

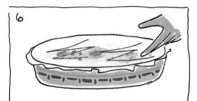

6. Cover with cling wrap. Cook on High 4 minutes.

7. Turn onions over. Spoon the sauce in the dish over.

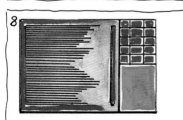

8. Cover. Cook on High 4 minutes Serve with parsley on top.

SWEET POTATO BAKE

Serves 4

about 400 g sweet potato
2 tablespoons honey
½ cup pineapple juice
1 teaspoon ground
   cinnamon
1 teaspoon grated lemon
   rind
30 g butter

1  Peel sweet potato. Cut it into thin slices.	**2**  Put honey, juice, cinnamon rind + butter in a bowl.	**3**  Cook it on High for 2 minutes.
4  Arrange sweet potato slices in a 20 cm casserole.	**5**  Pour the hot liquid all over sweet potato.	**6**  Cover with cling wrap. Cook on High for 8 minutes.
7 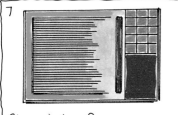 Stir gently. Cover + cook on High for 7 minutes.	**8**  Stand, covered, for 5 minutes, then serve.	*Although microwave energy ceases the moment food is removed from the oven, the food continues to cook for a short time, this is why some recipes call for a standing time.*

SCALLOPED POTATOES

Serves 4

4 medium potatoes
1 small onion
ground pepper
½ cup milk
¾ cup grated Cheddar
    cheese
sweet paprika

1. Peel the potatoes. Slice them thinly.

2. Peel the onion. Chop finely.

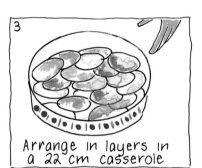

3. Arrange in layers in a 22 cm casserole

4. Sprinkle pepper over. Pour milk over it all.

5. Scatter grated cheese + paprika over top.

6. Cover casserole. Cook on High for 6 minutes.

7. Uncover. Cook on Medium (50%) 6 minutes.

8. Stand, covered, for 5 minutes, then serve.

ASIAN VEGETABLES

Serves 6

2 medium carrots
2 tablespoons oil
1 teaspoon grated green
   ginger
2 sticks celery
2 spring onions

2 medium zucchini
1 cup broccoli florets
1 tablespoon soy sauce
¼ cup water
¼ teaspoon chicken stock
   powder

Vegetables, like cauliflower and broccoli, are often cut into florets. This culinary term means cutting the small flower-like pieces of these vegetables into small segments.

1. Scrape carrots. Slice thinly on the diagonal. Put in large casserole.

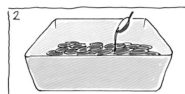

2. Add oil and ginger. Cover with cling wrap. Cook on High for 4 minutes.

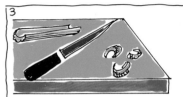

3. Slice the celery, diagonally into pieces 2cm long.

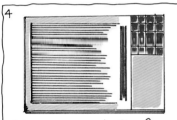

4. Add to casserole. Stir. Cover. Cook on High 3 minutes.

5. Slice spring onions and zucchini diagonally.

6. Add to casserole. Add broccoli. Stir gently

7. Mix soy sauce, water and stock. Pour over. Stir.

8. Cover with cling wrap. Cook on High 4 minutes.

FRENCH VEGETABLES

Serves 4

1 onion
1 teaspoon oil
½ green capsicum
3 zucchini
3 tomatoes
½ teaspoon dried basil
ground pepper

1

Peel onion. Chop finely. Put in large casserole.

2

Add oil. Cover Cook on High for 2 minutes.

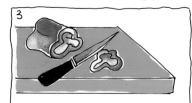

3

Chop up the green capsicum. Discard the seeds.

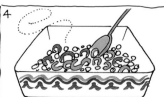

4

Stir in to casserole. Cover. Cook on High 2 minutes.

5

Slice zucchini thinly. Peel + chop tomatoes.

6

Add to the casserole. Stir in the basil

7

Cover with cling wrap. Cook on High 6 minutes.

8

Gently stir in pepper. Serve.

CREAMY BEANS

Serves 6

TOPPING
15 g butter
¼ cup dry breadcrumbs
2 tablespoons grated
   Cheddar cheese

440 g tin sliced green
   beans
½ cup tinned mushroom
   soup
¼ cup milk

Not all micro cooked dishes are covered during cooking, this helps some dishes to remain crispy and crunchy.

1
TOPPING:
Put butter in small bowl. Melt on High about 40 seconds.

2
Add crumbs + cheese. Stir. Set aside for Step 7.

3
Drain beans well. Put in a dish.

4
Mix soup + milk well in a jug.

5
Pour over beans.

6
Cover with cling wrap. Pierce. Cook on High 5 minutes.

7
Stir. Sprinkle the topping over.

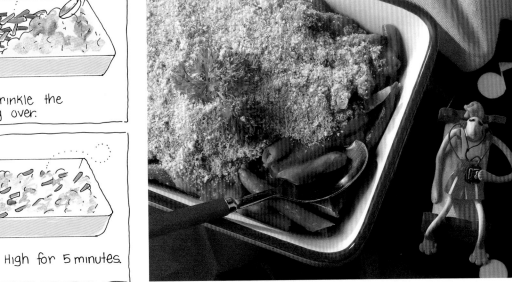

8
Cook on High for 5 minutes. Serve.

ZUCCHINI BAKE

Serves 4

1 small onion, sliced
15 g butter
3 zucchini
ground pepper

1 tomato, sliced thinly
½ cup grated Cheddar
  cheese
½ teaspoon sweet paprika

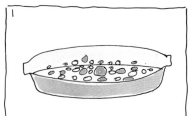

1. Put sliced onion + butter in shallow dish.

2. Cover with absorbent towel. Cook on High 2 minutes.

3. Rinse zucchini. Pat dry. Slice them thinly.

4. Put in dish. Add pepper. Stir it all together.

5. Cover with cling wrap. Pierce. Cook on High for 3 minutes.

6. Arrange tomato slices on top.

7. Sprinkle grated cheese + paprika evenly over.

8. Cook (uncovered) on High for 2 minutes more.

SAUCY CAULIFLOWER

Serves 6

375 g cauliflower pieces
¾ cup grated Cheddar
    cheese
25 g butter
3 tablespoons plain flour
ground pepper
1¼ cups milk
¼ cup grated Cheddar
    cheese (extra)

TOPPING
25 g butter
½ cup dry breadcrumbs

1 Put cauliflower in one layer in 20 cm round dish.

2 Sprinkle with the ¾ cup of grated cheese.

3 Chop up butter. Put in jug. Add flour, pepper + milk.

4 Cook on High for 2 minutes or till it boils. Whisk well.

5 Pour it all over. Sprinkle the extra grated cheese over.

6 Cover with cling wrap. Pierce. Cook on High 10-12 minutes.

7 TOPPING:
Melt butter in a jug (about 30 seconds on High). Stir in crumbs.

8 Sprinkle over. Cook on High (uncovered). 4 minutes.

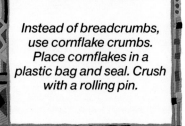

Instead of breadcrumbs, use cornflake crumbs. Place cornflakes in a plastic bag and seal. Crush with a rolling pin.

STEWED TOMATOES

Serves 6

500 g ripe tomatoes
1 teaspoon brown sugar
¼ teaspoon ground pepper
3 teaspoons cornflour
2 tablespoons cold water
1 tablespoon chopped
  parsley
a little dried basil

1
Chop up tomatoes.
Put into a 23 cm casserole.

2
Cover with cling wrap. Pierce.
Cook on High 5 minutes.

3
Take out. With tongs, carefully
remove tomato skins.

4
Sprinkle brown sugar
+ pepper over.

5
Mix cornflour + cold water
in a cup.

6
Stir into the tomatoes.
Stir in parsley.

7
Cook (uncovered) on High
for 2 minutes.

8
Sprinkle with basil.
stir gently + serve.

CHAPTER THREE

MAIN DISHES

Simply delicious main course dishes to make for the whole family. This chapter is full of easy recipes you can cook in just minutes in your microwave oven. Surprise your family with your culinary skills today.

CHICKEN FOR TWO

Serves 2

2 chicken breast fillets
2 slices bacon, rind removed
4 mushrooms, finely sliced
15 g butter
1 tablespoon soy sauce
1 tablespoon dry sherry

1 Pound chicken lightly with a mallet to flatten.

2 Lie it on a bacon slice and roll them up firmly.

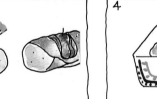

3 Push in a toothpick to hold it in place.

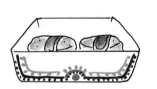

4 Put both in a small dish.

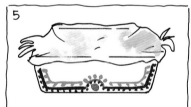

5 Cover with cling wrap. Pierce. Cook on High for 4 minutes.

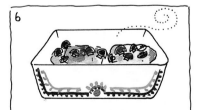

6 Turn chicken over. Sprinkle mushrooms over.

7 Add butter + soy sauce. Cover. Cook on High for 3 minutes.

8 Add sherry. Cover. Cook on Low (30% power) for 7 minutes.

CHICKEN CASSEROLE

Serves 4

4 chicken breast fillets
2 small potatoes, peeled + thinly sliced
1 teaspoon peeled + grated green ginger
1 tablespoon dry sherry
1 tablespoon soy sauce
1 teaspoon sugar

2 tablespoons cornflour
1 teaspoon chicken stock powder
¼ cup cold water
¾ cup hot water
6 mushrooms, sliced
¼ cup chopped parsley

Take great care when you uncover foods from the microwave oven to avoid burns. Lift the far side of the lid or covering up and away from you.

1 Chop chicken into bite-size pieces. Put in a bowl.

2 Add potato, ginger, sherry, soy sauce, sugar. Stir.

3 Mix cornflour, stock + cold water until smooth.

4 Whisk in hot water. Add to chicken. Stir it well.

5 Arrange evenly in a 25 cm wide dish.

6 Cook (uncovered) on High for 20 minutes. Stir once.

7 Scatter mushrooms + parsley over. Stir them through.

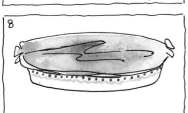
8 Cover with cling wrap. Cook on High 6 minutes.

CREAMY CHICKEN

Serves 6
6 chicken breast fillets
1 onion, finely chopped
½ cup sliced mushrooms
½ cup sliced celery
60 g butter
2 tablespoons plain flour
½ cup water

1 teaspoon sweet paprika
2 tablespoon dry sherry
2 egg yolks
½ cup milk
2 teaspoons chicken
 stock powder
1 cup canned whole kernel
 corn, drained

1 Put 3 chicken breasts in a round dish. Cover. Cook on High for 4 minutes.

2 Turn pieces over. Cover. Cook on High 2 minutes.

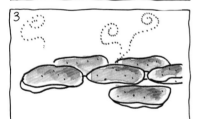

3 Do the same with rest of chicken. Set aside till cold.

4 Chop chicken fillets into small even-sized pieces.

5 Put onion, mushrooms, celery + butter in casserole. Cover. Cook on High for 5 minutes.

6 Whisk flour, water, paprika, sherry, egg yolks, milk and stock in a small bowl.

7 Stir in to casserole. Cover. Cook on High 2 minutes.

8 Stir well. Then stir in chicken pieces + corn. Cover. Cook on High for 4 minutes.

FISH & VEGETABLES

Serves 3

3 medium boneless white
  fish fillets (about 500 g)
2 tablespoons lemon juice
1 carrot
1 zucchini
1 slice bacon, rind
  removed
1 tablespoon soy sauce

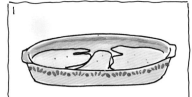

1 Put fish in one layer in a shallow dish

2 Sprinkle the lemon juice over.

3 Grate the carrot. Put it in a small bowl.

4 Grate zucchini. Put it in the bowl.

5 Chop up the bacon finely. Add to bowl.

6 Add soy sauce. Stir it together well.

7 Spread the mixture evenly on top of the fish.

8 Cook (uncovered) on High for 8 minutes.

SWEET 'N' SOUR FISH

Serves 3

3 medium boneless white
  fish fillets (about 500 g)
1 tablespoon lemon juice
1 cup Sweet 'n' Sour Sauce
  (see page 104)

1 Very lightly grease a shallow dish.

2 Arrange fish in one layer in the dish.

3 Sprinkle the lemon juice over.

4 Spread the Sweet 'n' Sour sauce evenly over.

5 Cover the dish with cling wrap. Pierce.

6 Cook it on High for 5 minutes.

7 Let it stand for 1 minute.

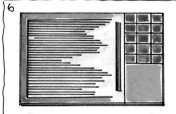

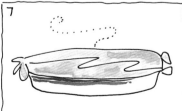

8 Carefully (it's hot!) remove cling wrap + serve.

FISH RISOTTO

Serves 4

15 g butter
1 small onion, finely
  chopped
1 cup uncooked long grain
  rice
2 teaspoons chicken stock
powder
1¾ cups boiling water
200 g tin smoked kipper
  fillets
½ cup frozen peas
2 tablespoons chopped
  parsley

1 Put butter + onion in 20 cm round casserole - 10 cm deep.

2 Cover with cling wrap. Prick. Cook on High 3 minutes.

3 Add rice. Stir. Cover. Cook on High 1 minute.

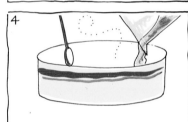

4 Add stock + boiling water. Stir. Cover with cling wrap. Prick.

5 Cook on High 8 minutes. Stand covered 4 minutes.

6 Drain fish well. Flake it with a fork.

7 Add fish + peas to rice. Stir it through.

8 Cook uncovered 2 minutes (High) Stir in parsley. Serve.

45

SPICY SAUSAGE

Serves 4

8 thin pork or beef
  sausages
1 cup hot water
½ green capsicum, finely
  chopped
1 onion, peeled + finely
  chopped
425 g tin of peeled
  tomatoes + juice
2 tablespoons chutney
½ teaspoon dried oregano
ground pepper

1

Put sausages in one layer in a large casserole.

2

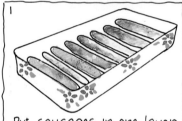

Add the 1 cup of hot water.

3

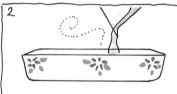

Cook (uncovered) on High for 10 minutes.

4

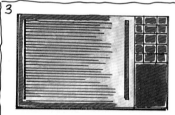

Drain sausages well. Cut them in half.

5

Put halved sausages back in the casserole.

6

Add capsicum, onion, whole tin of tomatoes.

7

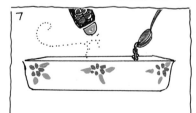

Add chutney, oregano, pepper. Stir gently.

This recipe is perfect with cooked spiral pasta or with taco chips, avocado and grated cheese.

8

Cook (uncovered) on High for 10 minutes. Stir gently and serve.

HAM STEAKS

Serves 3

1 tablespoon soy sauce
2 tablespoons chutney
2 tablespoons pineapple
   juice
3 ham steaks
1 green capsicum
1 cup tinned pineapple
   pieces

1

Put soy sauce, chutney + juice in a bowl + stir.

2

Pour into a 23 cm round dish.

3

Put the ham in, in one layer.

4

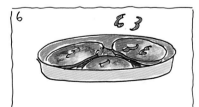

Turn each steak over to coat in the sauce.

5

Cut capsicum into thin strips. Throw seeds away.

6

Arrange capsicum on top of the ham.

7

Spread pineapple pieces on top of ham.

8

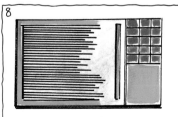

Cook on High (uncovered) for 7 minutes. Serve.

CABBAGE BAKE

Serves 4

3 cups shredded cabbage
2 tablespoons water
1 cup tinned tomatoes + juice
¼ cup grated cheese
1 cup shredded ham
1 tablespoon chopped parsley

1 Put cabbage + water in a 20 cm casserole.

2 Cover with cling wrap. Cook on High 6 minutes.

3 Roughly chop up the tinned tomatoes

4 Pour over hot cabbage. Stir gently.

5 Sprinkle with the grated cheese.

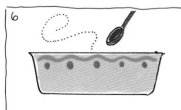

6 Stir the ham and parsley through.

7 Cover with cling wrap.

8 Cook it on High for 2 minutes. Stir + serve.

CRUNCHY TUNA

Serves 6

425 g tin of tuna, in brine
440 g tin of creamed
asparagus soup
3 hard boiled eggs,
chopped
1 cup frozen peas
1 cup potato crisps

1. Drain and flake tuna. Put it in a bowl.

2. Open tin of soup. Add to tuna. Stir.

3. Add chopped eggs and peas.

4. Mix it all together gently.

5. Spread it evenly in a 20 cm wide casserole.

6. Lightly crush crisps. Sprinkle on top.

7. Cover with absorbent paper. Cook on High 7½ minutes.

8. Serve on toast or with cooked rice.

MICROWAVE BREAKFAST

Making breakfast is easy if you use your microwave oven. In just about no time at all you can enjoy hot and scrumptious dishes like Herbed Eggs and Bacon or Fruity Porridge and for times when you are in a hurry Breakfast in a Muffin. Team these delicious meals with fresh juice or a hot milk drink for a perfect start to your day.

The following recipes all serve one.

FRUITY PORRIDGE

¼ cup rolled oats
¼ cup cold water
¼ cup milk
sultanas or raisins
milk and sugar, to serve

1 Place oats in a micro safe breakfast bowl. Add water and mix well. Cook on High (100%) for 1 minute.
2 Stir milk and sultanas into oats, cook on High (100%) 1 minute more or until porridge is thick. Serve with milk and sprinkle over a little sugar.

HERBED EGGS & BACON

1 teaspoon butter
2 eggs
2 tablespoons water
chopped chives
1 slice bacon, rind removed
toast and butter

1 Place butter in a micro safe dish, cook on High (100%) 20 seconds.
2 Whisk eggs, water and chives together. Pour eggs into bowl with the butter. Cover with cling wrap.
3 Cook on Medium (50%) 45 seconds. Stir well, cover again. Cook a further 45 seconds on Medium (50%). Stand covered while you cook your bacon.

4 Place bacon on a piece of absorbent paper on a plate, cover with another piece of absorbent paper. Cook on High (100%) 1 minute. Serve Herbed Eggs and Bacon with buttered toast.

Cover beaten eggs with cling wrap.

Cook on Medium (50%) 45 seconds, stir.

BREAKFAST IN A MUFFIN

1 English-style muffin
soft butter
1 egg
1 slice of ham

1 Place the muffin under a hot grill. Cook on each side until lightly golden and crisp.
2 When the muffin has cooled down a little carefully cut the muffin almost in half crosswise, leaving a little uncut on one side (this uncut piece becomes the 'hinge').
3 Carefully fold back the top and scoop out most of the crumbs. Spread butter on the inside of the muffin.
4 Break the egg into a small jug or glass and pour it into the muffin. Pierce the yolk two or three times with a toothpick.

5 Chop the ham into small pieces, sprinkle over the egg and close muffin.
6 Place the muffin on micro safe plate, cover with a piece of absorbent paper. Cook on High (100%) 1 minute, have a look inside the muffin to see how the egg is going and if it's not cooked give it another 10 seconds on High (100%).

Cut muffin in half, leaving a little uncut.

Pour egg into the hollowed out muffin.

CHEESY CROISSANTS

1 croissant
2 tablespoons grated Cheddar cheese

1 Carefully cut the croissant almost in half crosswise, fold back the top and sprinkle the cheese over the base. Fold top half of croissant over cheese.
2 Place croissant on a piece of absorbent paper. Place the croissant on the outer edge of the microwave oven turntable with the thickest part nearest the edge.
3 Cook on Low (30%) for 1 minute. Carefully remove from microwave and serve on a plate.

Cut the crossiant almost in half crosswise.

Place on absorbent paper to cook.

CHAPTER FOUR

Here we give some wonderfully rich desserts, all are quick to make. The hardest part is choosing your recipe, all are guaranteed to be perfectly sweet endings to any meal.

CUSTARD

Serves 4

3 tablespoons caster sugar
2 tablespoons custard
powder
1½ cups milk
2 egg yolks
1 teaspoon imitation vanilla
essence

1 Put sugar + custard powder in a 4 cup size bowl.

2 Add the milk and whisk it all well.

3 Cook on Medium (50%) for 3 minutes. Whisk well.

4 Cook on Medium (50%) for 4 minutes. Whisk well.

5 Add the egg yolks. Whisk well.

6 Cook on Medium (50%) for 1½ minutes, stirring twice.

7 Stir in the vanilla.

8 Serve hot or cold with fruits or puddings.

GOLDEN PEARS

Serves 6

1 tablespoon cornflour
¾ cup orange juice
1 tablespoon lemon juice
¼ cup brown sugar
¼ cup caster sugar
15 g butter
2 teaspoons grated orange
   rind
1 teaspoon grated lemon
   rind
425 g tin pear quarters
vanilla ice-cream

1

Put cornflour, orange and lemon juice in a bowl.

2

Whisk in brown + caster sugar, butter and rind.

3

Cook on High for 2 minutes. Whisk well.

4

Cook on High for 2 minutes more. Whisk.

5

Drain pears well.

6

Slice pears and place into a shallow casserole.

If you need to squeeze an orange or lemon, microwave it for 10 or 15 seconds on High (100%) and you'll get more juice than you would otherwise.

7

Pour the orange sauce over the pears.

8

Cook on High 2 minutes Spoon over ice-cream.

55

HOT FRUIT SALAD

Serves 6

2 bananas
310 g tin of peach slices,
  undrained
185 g tin of pineapple
  pieces, undrained

2 tablespoons brown sugar
1 tablespoon rum
vanilla ice-cream

1. Peel bananas. Slice into a 20 cm dish.

2. Open tin of peaches. Cut slices in half.

3. Pour syrup + peaches over bananas.

4. Empty whole tin of pineapple over

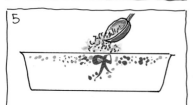

5. Sprinkle brown sugar over it all.

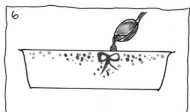

6. Add rum- don't stir it. leave bananas underneath

7. Cook it on High (uncovered) for 5 minutes.

8. Stir. Serve over scoops of vanilla ice-cream.

GLAZED APPLES

Serves 4

4 green cooking apples
2 tablespoons sultanas
2 tablespoons brown sugar
1 teaspoon cinnamon
30 g butter, cut in four
1 tablespoon golden syrup
1 tablespoon water
whipped cream

1

Carefully cut core from apples. Leave base in.

2

Peel thin strip of skin from round centre of apple.

3

Mix sultanas, brown sugar + cinnamon in a bowl.

4

Press firmly into apples. Put butter on top of each.

5

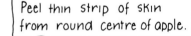

Put apples in dish. Add golden syrup + water.

6

Cook on High for 5 minutes.

7

Spoon syrup over apples. Cook on High 5 minutes.

8

Stand 3 minutes then serve with cream.

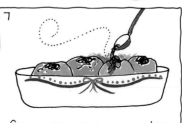

APPLE CRUMBLE

Serves 6

425 g tin pie apple filling
50 g butter
½ cup rolled oats
¼ cup plain flour
½ cup desiccated coconut
½ cup brown sugar
½ teaspoon cinnamon
cream or ice-cream

Spread apple in a 18cm wide pie dish.

2

Put the butter in a bowl.

3

Melt it on Medium (50%) for 40 seconds.

4

Stir in oats, flour, coconut, brown sugar + cinnamon

5

Spread evenly on top of apple.

6

Cook it on High for 5 minutes.

7

Allow to stand for 5 minutes.

8

Serve with cream or ice-cream.

PINEAPPLE CHEESECAKE

Serves 6-8

100 g butter
185 g plain sweet biscuits,
  crushed finely
250 g cream cheese
2 eggs
1 teaspoon grated lemon
  rind

2 tablespoons lemon juice
⅓ cup caster sugar
440 g tin crushed
  pineapple, drained
whipped cream

To crush sweet biscuits simply put them in a plastic food bag, twist to seal and lightly crush them with a meat mallet or rolling pin.

1
Melt butter on High for 1 minute. Stir in crumbs.

2
Press into base + sides of a 25 cm pie dish.

3
Cook on High for 1 minute. Set aside to cool.

4
Beat cream cheese, eggs, rind, juice + sugar till smooth.

5
Stir in the well drained pineapple.

6
Pour into the crumb crust.

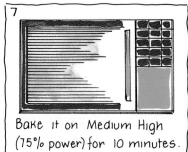

7
Bake it on Medium High (75% power) for 10 minutes.

8
Cool completely. Spread whipped cream on top.

RHUBARB BAKE

Serves 6

4 cups diced rhubarb
1 tablespoon tapioca
¾ cup caster sugar
1 teaspoon grated lemon
   rind
1 tablespoon water
cream or custard

1

Put rhubarb into a
20 cm casserole.

2

Sprinkle the tapioca
on top.

3
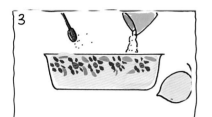
Sprinkle the sugar +
lemon rind over.

4

Add water. Cover with
cling wrap. Pierce.

5
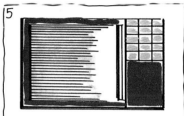
Cook it on HIGH for
5 minutes.

6

Take out and stir
gently.

7

Cover. Pierce. Cook on
Medium (50%) for 4 minutes.

8

Serve warm with
cream or custard.

PEAR CUSTARD

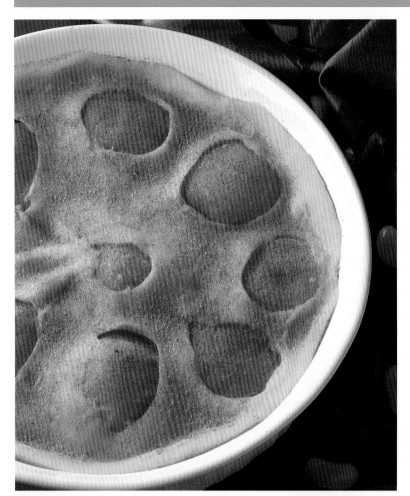

Serves 6

820 g tin pear halves
¼ cup caster sugar
2 tablespoons plain flour
3 eggs
1 tablespoon sweet sherry
½ cup milk
½ cup cream

1 Lightly grease a 23cm pie dish

2 Drain pears.

3 Arrange the pears in one layer in the dish.

4 Put the sugar + flour in a mixing bowl.

5 Add the eggs. Whisk until smooth.

6 Whisk in the sherry, milk + cream.

7 Pour evenly over the pears.

8 Cover with cling wrap. Pierce. Cook on High for 7 minutes.

BANANA TREAT

Serves 4

25 g butter
¼ cup brown sugar
½ teaspoon ground
   cinnamon
¼ cup cream
1 teaspoon grated lemon
   rind
1 cup tinned pineapple
   pieces, drained
2 tablespoons rum
3 bananas
vanilla ice-cream

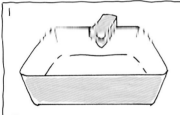

1

Put butter in 20cm casserole. Cook on High 30 seconds.

2

Whisk in sugar, cinnamon, cream and rind.

3

Cook on High 1½ minutes. Stir well.

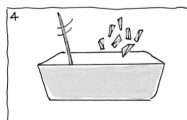

4

Stir in drained pine-apple and rum.

5

Peel and slice bananas. Stir them in.

6

Cook it (uncovered) on High for 3 minutes.

7

Stir very gently.

To make this recipe super scrumptious try adding chocolate bits and marshmallow.

8

Spoon over scoops of vanilla ice-cream. Luscious!

CHOC-ORANGE PUDDING

Serves 4

1 cup self-raising flour
1 tablespoon cocoa powder
½ cup caster sugar
½ cup milk
1 teaspoon imitation vanilla
   essence
25 g butter

SAUCE
1 tablespoon cocoa powder
1 tablespoon orange juice
¾ cup brown sugar
1½ cups water

cream

Never operate the microwave oven without food inside.

1
Grease a 20 cm casserole
Sift flour + cocoa into a bowl

2
Add sugar, milk and vanilla. Stir well.

3
Melt butter in small bowl on Medium (50%) for 1 minute.

4
Add to bowl. Mix well. Spread in casserole.

5
SAUCE:
Mix cocoa, juice, brown sugar, water in a jug. Stir well.

6
Pour evenly over pudding. DON'T STIR IT!

7
Cover with cling wrap. Pierce.

8
Cook it on High for 7 minutes. Stand 5 minutes Serve with cream.

CARROT PUDDING

Serves 6

125 g butter
1 cup grated carrot
440 g tin crushed
  pineapple, undrained
1 cup wholemeal plain flour
1 cup self-raising flour

½ teaspoon bicarbonate
  soda
¾ cup brown sugar
2 eggs
custard or cream

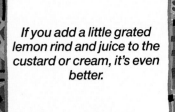

If you add a little grated lemon rind and juice to the custard or cream, it's even better.

1 Put butter in small bowl. Melt on Medium (50%) 2 minutes.

2 Put carrot + undrained tin of pineapple in a bowl.

3 Sift in both flours and bicarbonate soda. Mix well.

4 Add brown sugar, eggs + melted butter. Mix well.

5 Pour mixture into a large greased pudding bowl.

6 Cover with cling wrap. Pierce.

7 Cook on High for 8 to 10 minutes.

8 Stand 5 minutes. Turn out. Serve with custard or cream.

CHEESECAKE

Serves 6-8

100 g butter
185 g plain sweet biscuits, crushed finely
250 g cream cheese
¾ cup sour cream
2 eggs

½ cup caster sugar
2 teaspoons grated lemon rind
¼ cup lemon juice
whipped cream
sliced banana
passionfruit

1. Melt butter on High for 1 minute. Stir in crumbs.

2. Press firmly into base + sides of 25 cm pie dish.

3. Cook on High 1 minute. Set aside to cool.

4. Beat cream cheese + sour cream till smooth.

5. Add eggs, sugar, rind and juice. Beat well.

6. Pour into crumb crust spreading evenly.

7. Cook it on Medium (50%) for 10 minutes. Cool completely.

8. Spread with whipped cream, top with fruit and serve. Delicious!

CHAPTER FIVE

CAKES AND SLICES

Give family and friends a treat with these super baked goodies. Try your hand at Apple Cake, Sultana Slice or Fudge Squares. All of these cakes and slices are easy to make and to munch.

APPLE CAKE

Serves 6-8

125 g butter
½ cup brown sugar
2 tablespoons golden syrup
2 eggs
2 cups self-raising flour
2 teaspoons mixed spice
½ cup milk
2 green cooking apples

TOPPING
1 teaspoon caster sugar
1 teaspoon ground
   cinnamon

1
Grease a ring mould. Line base with baking paper.

2
Beat butter, sugar, syrup and eggs till smooth.

3
Sift in flour, + mixed spice.

4
Mix it in well adding milk at the same time.

5
Peel apples. Slice finely. Stir into the mixture.

6
Spread evenly in the ring.

7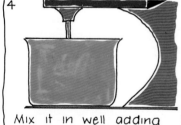
Cook on Medium High (75% power) for 12 minutes.

Sliced apples turn _____ if you don't use t____ straight away. To ____vent this squeeze som__ ____ juice over the____

8
Allow to stand for a few minutes, then turn it out, upside down. Sprinkle sugar + cinnamon on top. Serve warm with cream

PAVLOVA

Serves 6-8

4 egg whites (at room
    temperature)
1 cup caster sugar
½ teaspoon imitation vanilla
    essence
½ teaspoon vinegar
whipped cream + fruit

1. Beat the egg whites until soft peaks form.

2. Sprinkle in half the sugar. Beat well.

3. Slowly add rest of sugar. Beat until dissolved.

4. Add vanilla + vinegar. Beat in well.

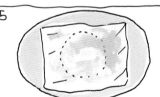

5. Take turntable out of oven. Put a sheet of baking paper on it. Mark an 18cm circle.

6. Spoon mixture onto paper. Form into a circle. Put back in the oven.

7. HIGH 2 minutes. door + leave it 10 minutes.

8. ● Carefully take it out ● of oven + leave until ❀ cold.❀ Carefully peel off the paper + put on ●● a plate. ●● Put whipped cream + fruit on.

CARAMEL FUDGE

Makes 18 pieces

1 cup icing sugar
2 cups brown sugar
1 tablespoon golden syrup
125 g butter
½ cup milk
¼ teaspoon cream of tartar
¼ cup chopped walnuts

1. Grease a 20cm square tin. Get out a deep 4 litre bowl.

2. Put icing sugar, brown sugar, golden syrup + butter in bowl

3. Add the milk and the cream of tartar. Stir.

4. Cook on High 5 minutes (uncovered) stirring once.

5. Cook on High 4 minutes - stir once after 2 minutes.

6. Stir in walnuts. Cook it on High 2 minutes more.

7. Beat well for 5 minutes until thick.

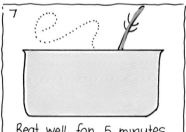

8. Pour into tin. Cut before it sets. Leave till cold.

FUDGE SQUARES

Makes 18 pieces

175 g butter
1 tablespoon golden syrup
¾ cup caster sugar
1 tablespoon cocoa powder
1½ cups plain flour
1½ teaspoons baking powder
¾ cup desiccated coconut
chocolate icing (see page 11)

1. Put butter, golden syrup, sugar, cocoa in big bowl.

2. Cook on Medium (50% power) for 2½ minutes.

3. Take out and stir really well.

4. Add sifted flour, baking powder + coconut. Stir well.

5. Press evenly into a glass casserole 20 cm square.

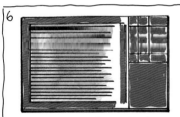
6. Cook on Medium High (75% power) for 8 minutes.

7. Ice with chocolate icing while still warm.

8. Leave until cold and then slice.

SULTANA SLICE

Serves 6-8

175 g butter
½ cup caster sugar
1 tablespoon golden syrup
½ cup sultanas
1 teaspoon grated lemon
  rind

2 cups plain flour
2 teaspoons baking
  powder
lemon icing (see page 11)

1. Put butter, sugar, golden syrup in a big bowl.

2. Cook it on Medium (50% power) 2 minutes.

3. Take out and stir well.

4. Add sultanas + lemon rind. Stir it well.

5. Sift in flour + baking powder. Mix well.

6. Spread evenly in a casserole 20 cm square.

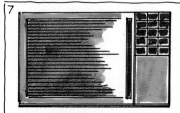

7. Cook on Medium High for 8 minutes.

8. Ice it with a lemon flavoured icing while still warm. Slice when completely cold

GINGER SLICE

Makes about 12 slices

125 g butter
¼ cup caster sugar
1 cup plain flour
½ teaspoon baking powder
½ teaspoon ground ginger

TOPPING
15 g butter
1 tablespoon golden syrup
½ teaspoon imitation vanilla
  essence
1 teaspoon ground ginger
⅓ cup icing sugar

Fruit cooked by microwave is sweeter and has better flavour than stewed fruit. Try cooking a single piece of fruit in its own skin, a peach maybe, but not for too long.

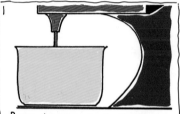

1. Beat butter and sugar until smooth.

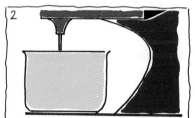

2. Sift in flour, baking powder + ginger. Mix it all well.

3. Mix to a dough. Knead until a smooth dough has formed.

4. Press firmly into 20cm casserole. Cook on Medium High (75% power) 6 minutes.

5. TOPPING:
Put butter + golden syrup in a bowl. Cook on High 30 seconds.

6. Stir in vanilla, ginger and icing sugar. Whisk well.

7. Spread it evenly over the hot base.

8. Leave it until cold and then slice.

DATE SLICE

Makes about 12 slices

1¼ cups self-raising flour
¾ cup caster sugar
1 cup desiccated coconut
1 cup chopped dates

¼ cup chopped walnuts
125 g butter
1 egg
1 tablespoon icing sugar

This luscious slice can be served for afternoon tea or cut into larger pieces and served with lashings of cream or ice-cream for dessert.

1. Sift flour into a large mixing bowl.

2. Stir in sugar, coconut, dates + walnuts.

3. Put butter in a small bowl. Melt it on Medium (50% power) for 2 minutes.

4. Add egg to butter. Whisk until combined.

5. Add to the flour mix in large bowl. Mix well.

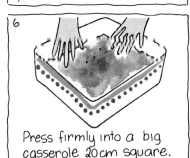

6. Press firmly into a big casserole 20cm square.

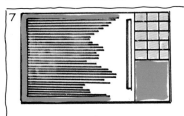

7. Cook on Medium High (75% power) 8½ minutes.

8. Leave until it's almost cold, then slice.
Leave in the dish. Let stand till completely cold. Dust with the icing sugar. Serve.

SCONE RING

Serves 6-8

30 g butter
2 tablespoons brown sugar
½ teaspoon ground
   cinnamon

¼ cup chopped walnuts
1¾ cups self-raising flour
15 g butter
¾ cup milk

1

Put butter in 20cm ring mould. Melt on Medium High (75% power) for 30 seconds.

2
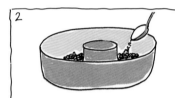
Sprinkle brown sugar, cinnamon + walnuts evenly over butter.

3

Sift flour into a bowl. Rub in the butter with fingers until it looks crumbly.

4

Add milk. Mix quickly to form a dough.

5

Knead the dough on a lightly floured surface.

6
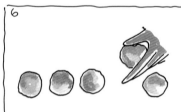
Break into 8 even-size pieces. Roll each into a ball.

7

Place the balls evenly in the ring mould.

8

Cook (uncovered) on High 2½-3 minutes. Stand for 2 minutes, then turn out.

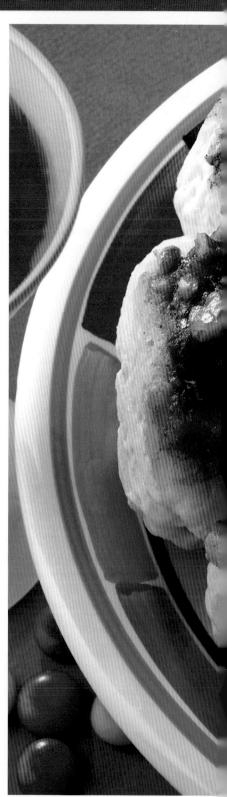

BANANA RING

Serves 6-8

125 g butter
¾ cup brown sugar
2 eggs
2 ripe bananas, mashed
1 teaspoon lemon juice
1 teaspoon grated lemon
   rind
1¼ cups self-raising flour
½ teaspoon baking powder
½ teaspoon ground
   cinnamon

1. Grease a 22cm micro ring mould of 5 cup capacity.

2. Line base neatly with a ring of baking paper. Grease the paper.

3. Beat butter, sugar, eggs. Mix in bananas, juice + rind.

4. Sift in flour, baking powder, + cinnamon. Mix well.

5. Spread evenly in dish.

6. Cook on Medium 4 minutes. Give dish a quarter turn.

7. Cook on High 4 minutes Stand for 10 minutes

Melt a little butter in a micro safe bowl for 20 or 30 seconds on High (100%) and use to grease micro safe cake dishes. It's easier if you use a pastry brush to grease the cake dish evenly.

8. Take out of dish. Cool. Ice with Lemon Icing (page 11), or top with banana.

PINEAPPLE CAKE

Serves 6-8

25 g butter
½ cup brown sugar
6 well drained pineapple
   rings
125 g butter
½ cup caster sugar
2 eggs
½ teaspoon almond
   essence
1¼ cups self-raising flour
¼ cup pineapple juice

1 Put the 25g butter in a 6·cup casserole. Cook on High for 1 minute

2 Sprinkle brown sugar evenly over butter.

3 Arrange pineapple rings on top of brown sugar.

4 Beat 125g butter, caster sugar, eggs + essence till smooth.

5 Sift in flour. Beat in with pineapple juice.

6 Spread carefully and evenly in casserole.

7 Cook it on High for 9 minutes.

Remember to clean up the kitchen when you have finished cooking, wash, dry and return all utensils to their place. Don't forget to wipe down your work surfaces.

8 Stand for 10 minutes. Turn out and serve.

CHAPTER SIX

SNACKS AND DRINKS

Microwave cooking is fun, especially when you cook these great microwave snacks and drinks. They are pefect for those in-between times when you want a tasty food fix fast.

GARLIC BREAD

Serves 6-8

1 loaf French bread (about
 60 cm long)
3 cloves garlic
100 g butter
ground pepper
1 tablespoon chopped
 parsley

1 Cut the French bread in half.

2 Slice 2 cm apart - don't cut through bottom crust.

3 Peel garlic cloves - crush them with flat side of knife.

4 Put crushed garlic in a small bowl. Add butter.

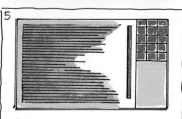

5 Soften butter - about 40 seconds on Low (30% power)

6 Add pepper, parsley. Mash well with a fork.

7 Spread butter evenly onto one side of each slice

8 Wrap each half loosely in wax paper.
Cook each half separately on High for 1 minute.

TUNA BURGERS

Serves 4

185 g tin of tuna, in brine
½ cup grated Cheddar cheese
¼ cup mayonnaise
1 tablespoon tomato sauce
1 tablespoon lemon juice
ground pepper
4 hamburger buns — halved
butter

1

Drain tuna well. Put it in a bowl.

2

Add cheese, mayonnaise, tomato sauce, + lemon.

3

Add pepper. Mix it all together well.

4

Butter the buns lightly.

5

Spread mixture evenly on 4 halves.

6

Put the top on each burger.

7

Wrap each one in absorbent paper.

8

Cook (2 at a time) on High for 1½ minutes.

PITTA SNACK

Serves 1

1 small pitta bread
2 teaspoons tomato paste
  (or chutney)
1 slice Swiss cheese
2 slices ham
1 teaspoon chopped spring
  onion

1 Put pitta bread on plate.

2 Spread with tomato paste or chutney.

3 Slice cheese thinly

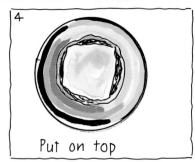

4 Put on top

5 Chop ham finely

6 Sprinkle over

7 Sprinkle chopped spring onion over.

8 Cook on High 30 seconds until cheese melts.

CHICKEN WINGS

Serves 4

10 chicken wings
¾ cup plum sauce
1 teaspoon brown sugar
2 teaspoons sesame seeds

1 Put wings in one layer in a dish.

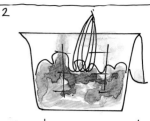

2 Mix plum sauce and brown sugar.

3 Pour it evenly over wings. Cover.

4 Stand 2 hours. Turn wings over once.

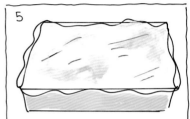

5 Cover with cling wrap. Pierce holes in it.

6 Cook on High for 6 minutes.

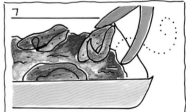

7 Turn wings over. Cook on Medium 5 minutes.

8 Stand 2 minutes. Sprinkle with seeds. Cool.

SCOTCH EGGS

Serves 4

450 g sausage mince
1 cup soft white
  breadcrumbs

1 tablespoon tomato sauce
4 hard boiled eggs, shelled
1 cup fine, dry breadcrumbs

1 Put sausage, soft crumbs, sauce in a bowl.

2 Mix it really well until smooth

3 Divide mixture into 4

4 With wet hands, fold + press it round each egg

5 Put fine crumbs in a dish Roll each one till coated.

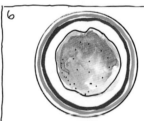

6 Put one egg at a time on a plate

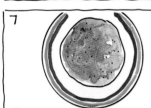

7 Cook on High 1 minute. Turn egg over and cook on High 1 minute.

8 Leave on absorbent paper until cold, then cut in half.

HAM & EGG ROLL

Serves 2

1 bread roll or English muffin
¼ cup grated Cheddar cheese
10 g butter
1 egg

1 tablespoon chopped parsley
ground pepper
2 tablespoons chopped ham

You can make this same recipe using baked potato halves instead of the roll.

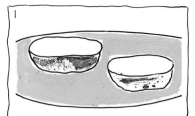

1. Cut roll in half. Put on plate cut side up.

2. Pull a little bread out of centre to make a cavity.

3. Put grated cheese in.

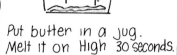

4. Put butter in a jug. Melt it on High 30 seconds.

5. Add egg, parsley, pepper. Whisk.

6. Pour it carefully into each half.

7. Sprinkle ham on top.

8. Cook on High 1¾ mins. till egg is puffy + cooked.

MUESLI BARS

Makes 12 pieces

1 cup desiccated coconut
1 cup unsalted peanuts
1 cup sunflower seeds
1 cup sesame seeds
1 cup rolled oats
125 g butter
½ cup brown sugar
¼ cup honey

1 Put coconut, peanuts, seeds oats in big, flat bowl.

2 Cook on High 6 minutes.

3 Put butter, sugar, honey in another bowl.

4 Cover with absorbent paper. Cook 4½ minutes on Medium (50%).

5 Stir well. Add to mix in big bowl. Stir well.

6 Spread evenly in a 20 cm x 30 cm tin.

7 Press down firmly with a cup.

8 Leave till cold, then slice into bars.

HOT CHOCOLATE

Serves 3

3 cups milk
⅓ cup grated dark
  chocolate
1 tablespoon sugar
½ teaspoon ground
  cinnamon
1 egg

1. Put milk in big jug. Cook on High 2 minutes.

2. Add chocolate, sugar + cinnamon. Whisk.

3. Whisk egg in a cup

4. Add to jug. Whisk.

5. Cook on High - about 3-4 minutes till foamy - don't boil it!

6. Whisk well.

7. Pour into 3 mugs.

8. Sprinkle with a little extra cinnamon. Serve.

COCOA MALLOW

Serves 1

½ teaspoon cocoa powder
1 teaspoon sugar
3 tablespoons hot water
about 1 cup of milk
1 white marshmallow

1. Put cocoa in a mug

2. Add sugar + hot water

3. Stir well.

4. Cook on High 30 seconds

5. Stir well.

6. Add milk to fill mug ¾ full.

7. Cook on High 90 seconds

8. Pop marshmallow on top.

SCRAMBLED EGGS

Serves 1

10 g butter
¼ cup milk
1 tablespoon chopped
   parsley
2 eggs
toast

1 Put butter in a 2 cup size jug.

2 Cook on High 10-20 seconds till melted.

3 Add milk, parsley, eggs.

4 Mix it with a fork.

5 Cook on High 1 minute. Stir gently with fork.

6 Cook 1 minute more. Watch it, when egg swells, take out.

7 Stir it gently.

8 Stand 1 minute. Serve with buttered toast.

CAPPUCCINO

Serves 4

2 cups milk
4 teaspoons grated
   chocolate
4 teaspoons sugar
2 teaspoons instant coffee
⅓ cup cream, whipped
ground cinnamon

1. Put milk in a 4-cup glass jug.

2. Cook on High 3–3½ minutes till hot but not boiling.

3. Add grated chocolate + sugar. Stir it well.

6. Top with cream.

4. Stir in instant coffee. Stir very well.

7. Sprinkle cinnamon on.

5. Pour into 4 mugs.

8. Serve with cookies.

FUN GINGERBREAD MEN

A great way to spend a rainy morning or afternoon is to cook up a batch of gingerbread men. It will take a little while to get everything organised but only a minute or two to turn out your first cooked gingerbread man after the dough is prepared and cut to shape. You may find that the dough can get rather sticky if handled too much and is difficult to mould so ask an adult or an older brother or sister to help.

GINGERBREAD MEN CHECKLIST

1   Collect all the things you will need to make the gingerbread men:
- A gingerbread man (GBM) cutter — we've used a plastic one about 13 cm from head to toe (available from kitchenware departments).
- A roll of special baking paper — great for non-stick rolling out of dough.
- A small bottle of Parisian essence to give the GBM good colour.
- A little space in the refrigerator for chilling the pastry.

- If possible some freezer space for the cut-out GBM. Partially frozen they are much easier to handle.
- An egg slice for lifting and handling the GBM.
- A small, flat-bladed knife or spatula to gently press and flatten any 'bubbles' that appear on the cooked GBM when they come out of the microwave oven.

2   If you'd rather make 'Funny Faces' instead of gingerbread men (they are easier than GBM and taste just the same), then you will need a large mug or small bowl with a diameter of about 8 cm. Place one of these upside-down over the rolled out pastry and using a small, sharp pointed knife, cut out circles which can then be cooked in the same way as the GBM.

3   To decorate 'Funny Faces': Spread butter icing evenly over each and use sweets, licorice, glacé cherries, jelly beans and coloured sprinkles to make eyes, nose and mouth.

NOTE: Make sure there are no lumps of brown sugar still undissolved when it is mixed with the butter. Microwaves are attracted to sugar and you could find that over-browning or even burning could occur if these lumps are present. Remove any really stubborn lumps that refuse to melt.

To avoid uneven cooking, it is best to have a fresh mug, ¾ filled with cold water, in the oven for each cooking period for the GBM.

GINGERBREAD MEN IN THE MICROWAVE

Makes about 24

125 g butter, softened slightly (not melted)
¾ cup brown sugar, well packed
1 x 60 g egg
1 teaspoon Parisian essence (optional, for colour)
2 cups plain flour
2 tablespoons ground ginger

1   Put butter in small bowl and if you have an electric mixer, beat the butter on medium speed until it is light and fluffy. Add brown sugar, beat until it is well mixed with butter and no sugar lumps are visible. Add the egg and Parisian essence, mix on a slightly lower speed until well combined.

2   Now you'll have to scrape the mixture into a larger bowl. Stir through the flour, sifted with ground ginger, by hand. The dough should be fairly firm, not sticky. However, as you need to use your hands to press it together, it could eventually become a little sticky. Don't worry if this happens — just divide the dough in half, form two balls and press each flat to about 3 cm thickness and wrap in greaseproof or baking paper and put in the refrigerator for about 30 minutes.

3   Now roll out one of the batches of pastry between two sheets of baking paper until it is about 5 mm thick. Remove the top sheet of baking paper and, using the cutter, cut out as many GBM as you can from the dough. Carefully remove the left-over pastry pieces in between the figures, but if this means spoiling the figures, leave this job until after chilling. Now carefully slide the figures with the baking paper onto a flat biscuit tray and place in the freezer.

4   When they are quite firm and easy to pick up with an egg slice or spatula, place two at a time on a piece of baking paper. Put them in the microwave oven along with a large mug, three-quarters full of water, and cook on High (100%) for 1 or 1½ minutes or until they are crisp when allowed to cool. If the GMB are even just a little soft on cooling, return them for a few more seconds until they stay really crisp when cool.

1 Roll out pastry between two sheets of baking paper.

2 Cook in microwave oven with mug of water.

3 Butter icing: The mixture should be soft but not runny.

BUTTER ICING

You'll need a piping bag and a writing icing tube (not too fine a tube — it makes it harder to push the icing out through a very small hole). If you don't have a piping bag, you can easily spread the butter icing over the gingerbread men with a small spatula. Decorate with small sweets.

40 g butter
1 cup icing sugar, sifted
2 teaspoons of milk (approximately)

1   Place the butter in a micro safe bowl and heat on High (100%) for a few seconds, until the butter melts. Stir in the sifted icing sugar, add enough milk to make the mixture soft but not runny and beat.

2   Fill a small piping bag with butter icing and carefully pipe the icing around the gingerbread men to form eyes, nose, mouth and clothing.

NOTE: This is an easy-to-make icing and easy to use for decorating your GBM. Because it starts off with melted butter and the icing sugar is added along with a little milk, it is easy to draw with. On a cool day the icing will begin to set a little as the butter cools down. At this stage the left-over icing in the bowl may need a little gentle heat to make it run free — this would mean just a couple of seconds in the microwave on High — be careful not to over-heat it. However, even holding the bag of icing will often be enough for the butter to warm up just a little and make it easy to squeeze out the icing.

CHAPTER SEVEN

JAMS AND CHUTNEY

Make the most of your microwave with these simple jam, chutney and sauce recipes. The jams and chutneys make great gift ideas and the sauces will liven up any meal.

LEMON BUTTER

Makes 2 cups

½ cup lemon juice
75 g butter
1¼ cups caster sugar
2 teaspoons grated lemon
   rind
4 eggs

1 Put juice and butter into a bowl.

2 Cook it on High for 1½ minutes.

3 Whisk in the sugar and lemon rind.

4 Add the eggs and whisk well.

5 Cook on High for 7 minutes. Remove from oven.

6 Whisk well for 1 or 2 minutes.

7 Pour into 2 hot, dry, clean jars. Cover when cold.

8 Store in refrigerator.

MARMALADE

Makes 1½ cups

1 carrot
1 orange
2 lemons
1¾ cups water
4 cups sugar

1 Peel + chop carrot. Chop orange + lemons - don't peel.

2 Put half in blender. Add ½ cup water. Blend 30 seconds.

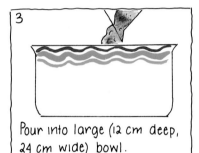

3 Pour into large (12 cm deep, 24 cm wide) bowl.

4 Blend rest of fruit with another ½ cup of water.

5 Add to bowl. Add sugar and rest of water. Cover loosely.

6 Cook on High for 10 minutes. Stir well. Be careful, very hot.

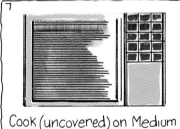

7 Cook (uncovered) on Medium for 30 minutes. Stir well.

8 Pour into hot, sterilised jars. Seal when cold.

STRAWBERRY JAM

Makes 2 cups

500 g strawberries, twist to
    remove green leafy ends
    and stalks
¼ cup lemon juice
2 cups sugar

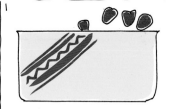

1

Put strawberries in big bowl
24 cm wide, 12 cm deep.

2

Cover with cling wrap. Pierce.
Cook on High for 4 minutes.

3

Mash the strawberries
to a pulp.

4

Add lemon juice and the
sugar. Stir well.

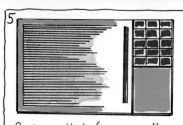

5

Cook on High (uncovered)
20 minutes. Stir now + again.

6

Watch it! Turn to Medium
(50%) if it looks like boiling over.

7

Let stand for 5 minutes.
Stir.

8

Pour into hot, sterilised jars.
When cool seal and label.

TOMATO CHUTNEY

Makes 3 cups

750 g ripe tomatoes
2 onions, peeled +
   chopped
1 cup white vinegar
1½ cups sugar
2 teaspoons curry powder
2 teaspoons French
   mustard
2 teaspoons salt
¼ cup cornflour
¼ cup cold water

1. Chop tomatoes in quarters, remove core. Put in big bowl – 24 cm wide + 12 cm deep.

2. Add onions, vinegar, sugar, curry, mustard + salt. Stir well.

3. Cover with cling wrap. Cook it on High for 10 minutes.

4. Stir. Remove tomato skins with tongs. Take your time!

5. Cook (uncovered) on High for 10 minutes.

6. Mix cornflour + cold water till smooth. Stir in well.

7. Cook (uncovered) on High 6 minutes. Let stand 5 minutes.

8. Stir. Pour into hot, sterilised jars. Seal when cold. Refrigerate.

Jars for chutney and jams must be sterilised. To do this clean jars thoroughly and warm them in a conventional oven at 150°C. Using oven mitts remove jars from the oven and fill.

SWEET 'N' SOUR SAUCE

Makes 1 cup

1 onion
1 carrot
¼ cup water
3 tablespoons cornflour
2 tablespoons soy sauce
¼ cup brown sugar
¼ cup white vinegar

¼ cup tomato sauce
¾ cup water
1 teaspoon chicken stock
   powder
2 tablespoons dry sherry
¼ cup pineapple juice
1 cup pineapple pieces

Take great care when cooking sauces, jams and chutneys as these foods can be very hot. Use oven mitts when handling dishes or ask an adult to help.

1. Peel + slice onion. Scrape carrot + cut into matchsticks.

2. Put in bowl with the ¼ cup water. Cover with cling wrap.

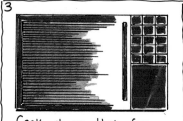

3. Cook it on High for 4 minutes.

4. Put cornflour, soy sauce in a large measuring jug.

5. Whisk in brown sugar, vinegar, tomato sauce, water, stock, sherry and juice.

6. Add to onion + carrot in bowl. Stir well.

7. Cook (uncovered) on High for 4 minutes, stirring twice.

8. Stir in pineapple. Cook on High for 1½ minutes more.

CHEESE SAUCE

Makes 2 cups

50 g butter
¼ cup plain flour
2 cups milk
½ cup grated Cheddar
   cheese
ground pepper

1 Put butter in a bowl. Cover with absorbent paper.

2 Cook on Medium (50% power) for 2 minutes till melted

3 Add the flour. Stir in well.

4 Add the milk. Whisk it in well.

5 Cook (uncovered) on High for 2 minutes. Whisk well.

6 Cook on High for 3½ minutes, whisking once.

7 Stir in cheese + pepper Stir well.

8 Serve spooned over hot vegetables.

PLUM SAUCE

1

Put plum jam in a bowl.

2

Add tomato sauce.

Makes 1 cup

¼ cup plum jam
¼ cup tomato sauce
¼ cup brown sugar
¼ cup soy sauce
1 teaspoon French Mustard
2 teaspoons
   Worcestershire sauce

3

Stir in brown sugar and soy sauce.

4

Stir in mustard and Worcestershire sauce.

5

Whisk it all well.

6

Cook (uncovered) on High for 2 minutes.

7

Whisk again.

8

Serve over chops or sausages.

CARAMEL SAUCE

Makes 1 cup

125 g butter
1 cup brown sugar
1 cup water
2 tablespoons golden syrup
3 tablespoons cornflour
¼ cup cream
ice-cream

Put butter + brown sugar into a bowl.

Cook 2 minutes on Medium (50% power).

Stir it really well.

Add water, golden syrup, cornflour. Whisk well.

Cook it on Medium (50% power) for 3 minutes.

Take out + add cream. Whisk well. Cook on High for 2 minutes.

Stir well. Stand 5 minutes

Serve warm or cold over ice-cream.

USEFUL INFORMATION

The recipes in this book are all thoroughly tested,
using standard metric measuring cups and spoons.
All cup and spoon measurements are level.
We have used eggs with an average weight of 55 g each
in all recipes.

WEIGHTS AND MEASURES

In this book, metric measures and their imperial equivalents have been rounded out to the nearest figure that is easy to use. Different charts from different authorities vary slightly; the following are the measures we have used consistently throughout our recipes.

OVEN TEMPERATURE CHART

	°C	°F	Gas Mark
Very slow	120	250	½
Slow	150	300	1–2
Mod. slow	160	325	3
Moderate	180	350	4
Mod. hot	190	375	5–6
Hot	200	400	6–7
Very hot	230	450	8–9

LENGTH

Metric	Imperial
5 mm	¼ in
1 cm	½ in
2 cm	¾ in
5 cm	2 in
8 cm	3 in
10 cm	4 in
12 cm	5 in
15 cm	6 in
20 cm	8 in
25 cm	10 in
30 cm	12 in
46 cm	18 in
50 cm	20 in
61 cm	24 in

CUP AND SPOON MEASURES

A basic metric cup set consists of 1 cup, ½ cup, ⅓ cup and ¼ cup sizes.

The basic spoon set comprises 1 tablespoon, 1 teaspoon, ½ teaspoon and ¼ teaspoon.

1 cup	250 mL/8 fl oz
½ cup	125 mL/4 fl oz
⅓ cup	80 mL/
(4 tablespoons)	2½ fl oz
¼ cup	
(3 tablespoons)	60 mL/2 fl oz
1 tablespoon	20 mL
1 teaspoon	5 mL
½ teaspoon	2.5 mL
¼ teaspoon	1.25 mL

LIQUIDS

Metric	Imperial
30 mL	1 fl oz
60 mL	2 fl oz
100 mL	3½ fl oz
125 mL	4 fl oz (½ cup)
155 mL	5 fl oz
170 mL	5½ fl oz (⅔ cup)
200 mL	6½ fl oz
250 mL	8 fl oz (1 cup)
300 mL	9½ fl oz
375 mL	12 fl oz
410 mL	13 fl oz
470 mL	15 fl oz
500 mL	16 fl oz (2 cups)
600 mL	1 pt (20 fl oz)
750 mL	1 pt 5 fl oz (3 cups)
1 litre (1000 mL)	1 pt 12 fl oz (4 cups)

DRY INGREDIENTS

Metric	Imperial
15 g	½ oz
30 g	1 oz
45 g	1½ oz
60 g	2 oz
75 g	2½ oz
100 g	3½ oz
125 g	4 oz
155 g	5 oz
185 g	6 oz
200 g	6½ oz
250 g	8 oz
300 g	9½ oz
350 g	11 oz
375 g	12 oz
400 g	12½ oz
425 g	13½ oz
440 g	14 oz
470 g	15 oz
500 g	1 lb (16 oz)
750 g	1 lb 8 oz
1 kg (1000 g)	2 lb

GLOSSARY

capsicum = sweet pepper
cornflour = cornstarch
flour = use plain all purpose
 unless otherwise
 specified
eggplant = aubergine
spring onion = shallot
zucchini = courgettes

INDEX

Published by Murdoch Books, a division of Murdoch Magazines Pty Ltd,
213 Miller Street, North Sydney, NSW 2060

Author: Mary Pat Fergus
Murdoch Books Food Editor: Jo Anne Calabria
Design and Finished Art: Jayne Hunter
Photography: Jon Bader
Illustrations: Mary Pat Fergus Jayne Hunter
Food Stylist: Marie Hélène Clauzon
Border Artwork: Jan Gosewinckel
Index: Michael Wyatt

Publisher: Anne Wilson
Publishing Manager: Mark Newman
Production Manager: Catie Ziller
Managing Editor: Sarah Murray
Marketing Manager: Mark Smith
National Sales Manager: Keith Watson

National Library of Australia Cataloguing-in-Publication Data
Fergus, Mary Pat
Kid's microwave cookbook
Includes index.
ISBN 0 86411 258 0

1. Microwave cookery — Juvenille literature I. Title.

641.5882

First Published 1992
Printed by Toppan Printing Co. Ltd, Singapore
Typeset by Adtype, Sydney

Distributed in the UK, by Australian Consolidated Press (UK) Ltd,
20 Galowhill Road, Brackmills, Northampton NN4 OEE
Enquiries — 0604 760456